Qetoret

The Fragrance of Prayer

Rebecca Park Totilo

Table of Contents

The Archeological Discovery

In an article entitled, "The Spiritual Significance of the *Qetoret* (Incense) in Ancient Jewish Tradition," author Rabbi Avraham Sutton describes the momentous archeological discovery of the Holy Incense:

"In March 1988, Vendyl Jones and his team of *Bnei Noah* volunteers found a clay juglet about five inches in height in a cave in Qumran, just west of the northern end of the *Yam HaMelach* (Dead Sea). The juglet contained a reddish oil. It is believed to be the only surviving sample of the balsam oil that was prescribed in the Torah for anointing the *Mishkan* (Tabernacle) and its vessels, as well as the *Cohanim*-Priests and Kings of Israel. The oil, when found, had a honey-like consistency. The juglet in which it was found was wrapped in palm leaves and carefully concealed in a 3-foot deep pit which preserved it from looting and the extreme climatological extremes of the area.

In April 1992, Vendyl and his team discovered 600 kilos of "reddish-brown organic substance" in a carefully sealed rock silo in another part of the Qumran cave complex. Subsequent palynological analysis determined that this reddish-brown substance contains traces of at least eight of the eleven spices that were used in the manufacture of the *Pitum HaQetoret* (Incense Mixture) and burned in the Temple.

In 1994, the incense spices were presented to Rabbi Yehudah Getz of blessed memory, late Chief Rabbi of the Western Wall and Holy Places in Israel. A sample was also given to Rabbi Ovadiah Yoseph. Rabbi Ovadiah had his own chemist analyze the mixture to confirm its organic nature. Then both rabbis requested that Vendyl Jones "burn" some of the incense for scientific purposes (not with fire but with hydrochloric acid). At their suggestion, he had the spices combined together with the Sodom Salt and Karshina Lye which were also found stored separately in the cave in Qumran.

The results were astonishing. Although the spices had lost some of their potency over the two millennia since their burial, it was still powerful. The residue of its fragrance lingered in the vicinity for several days following the experiment. Several people present reported that their hair and clothing retained the aroma. More amazing, the area in which the spices were burned changed. It had been infested with a variety of flies, ants, moths and other insects. After the *Qetoret* was burned, no sign of these pests was seen for quite a while. This is reminiscent of the *Mishnah* in *Avot* (5:5) which states that there were no flies in the area of the Temple, nor was a snake or scorpion ever able to harm anyone anywhere in Jerusalem as long as the Temple stood.

Rabbi Avraham Sutton stated he work with Vendyl Jones in 1995 and met Avraham Sand of Tiferet International Aromatherapy, a master perfumer who was able to authenticate and obtain nine of the original eleven incense spices and reproduce them in the form of essential oils. In essence, Sand was able to parallel Vendyl's discoveries of both the Anointing Oil and *Qetoret* in Qumran. His work was supervised under the rabbinical guidance of Rabbi Menachem Burstein, the foremost Jewish authority on the botany and chemistry of Temple artifacts. This was done in order to sidestep the strict prohibition against experimentation with the various plant materials in their original form. Rabbi Burstein advised him that there is no prohibition whatsoever against enjoying the essential oil extracts of these same botanicals.

"By getting back in touch with the mystery of the *Qetoret*, and unearthing its ancient secrets," Rabbi Avraham suggests, "we can awaken something else in ourselves that is sorely needed at this time."

Temple Service

The burning of the קְטֹרֶת _Qetoret_ (Holy Incense) was central to all of the ceremonies conducted in the Temple as a key component required under the Law of Moses. Situated near the Arabian Peninsula along the spice route, large amounts of incense could easily be imported, where Israelites were well acquainted with the use of incense in religious worship having coming from the land of Egypt.

When Moses received instruction to build the tabernacle he was told to include an altar on which his brother Aaron was to burn incense every morning and every evening throughout all of Israel's generations. Each morning when the menorah was cleaned and each evening when the lamp was lit, a priest burned the _Qetoret_ (Holy Incense) on the small Golden Altar in the center of the sanctuary (Exodus 30:8).

The altar of incense, upon which the priests burned the Holy Incense was made of shittim wood, overlaid with gold and had four horns upon its corner, similar to Canaanite altars found in Palestine.

Incense in a covered vessel called a _Bazach_ was brought in by the _Cohen_ and placed inside another spoon-like vessel called a _Kaf_ then covered with a cloth. A second _Cohen_ performed the Avodah of the *Mahtah* (the pan), which the priest carried in his hand.

Aaron carried the incense using a pan he offered for the sins of the people in Numbers 17:11-12. Both of Aaron's sons had his own pan (Leviticus 10:1) as well as the insubordinate Levites who sacrificed incense on pans, which were used afterward to cover the altar of burnt offering of the Tabernacle (Numbers 17:4). Apparently, every priest had his own censer.

Using tongs or a golden censer, the priests removed hot coals from the altar of sacrifice and placed them upon the altar of incense twice daily, after which the incense would be sprinkled upon. The prominent position of the altar of incense in the Holy Place was directly before the veil of the tabernacle or Temple.

A special offering of incense was made on the Day of Atonement (Leviticus 16:12-13), in which the *Cohen Gadol* (High Priest) entered the Holy Place, carrying in his right hand the pan for the incense, filled with live coals, and in his left hand the spoon-like *kaf*, containing the incense. After placing both of these utensils on the floor, the High Priest took the incense from the *kaf* with the hollow of his hand, and heaped it upon the pan containing the coals (Leviticus 16:12).

The High Priest then placed blood from the sacrifice upon the four horns of the altar of incense, foreshadowing the time when Yeshua, our High Priest would offer his own life for the sins of all mankind. Then the High Priest entered the Holy of Holies, where he burned incense in a gold censer, just as our Messiah is in the presence of Yahweh on His throne in Heaven (Hebrew 9:6-15).

The Rabbis teach that the incense that was compounded weighed: 368 *maneh* [measures] - 365 of these corresponded to the number of days in the solar year, one measure a day, half in the morning and half towards evening. Once a year, a new batch was prepared, allowing for one *maneh* (approximately five pounds) to be burnt twice daily, once as part of the *Shacharit* (morning) service and once as part of the *Mincha / Musaf* (afternoon) service. Three *manot* were reserved for Yom Kippur. Any amount leftover after Yom Kippur, the amount used being dependent on the size of each High Priest's hand (Leviticus 16:12), was added to the next year's batch. Every 70 years or so, enough excess accumulated to require only half the amount of *Qetoret* be prepared.

The other three measures were those that the *Cohen Gadol* or High Priest would bring into the Holy of Holies as a double handful on Yom Kippur. He would replace them in the mortar on the eve of Yom Kippur and regrind them thoroughly to make the *Qetoret* compound extra fine.

In addition to the daily burning of incense, incense was added to sacrifices, such as the meat and flour offerings. The incense offering was omitted only in two cases - with the sin offering of the poor (Leviticus 5:11-13) and with the meat offering of the lepers (Leviticus 14:10, 20).

Like the cloudy pillar from which Yahweh spoke to the children of Israel during the Exodus, the burning incense rose in a pillar of smoke before the ark from which Yahweh communed with the priest.

As it was then, so it is today. God can only be approached through prayer, with a sincere heart of thanksgiving and worship. Prayer, like incense is the power to pierce through the darkness of hopelessness and take us into the very presence of God.

From the altar of sacrifice, our savior who suffered and offered himself as the perfect sacrifice did so willingly, so we could have accessed to the Father. The altar where the incense was burnt, located before the mercy seat, represents Yahweh's throne and our High Priest, Yeshua Ha Mashiach, who has access because of the rent veil (Matthew 27:31), continues to make intercession on our behalf before the Father.

Allow the coals of the *Ruach Ha Kodesh* (Holy Spirit) to burn away the dross and sin that hinders communion with God. He will reveal those things we should pray and what we should ask, according to His will.

Holy Incense

In the Torah we find the commandment concerning the *Qetoret* immediately following the Anointing Oil:

> Yahweh said to Moses: Take for yourself spices -- stacte, onycha, galbanum, [as well as other specified] spices, and pure frankincense -- equal amounts of each. [Grind each spice separately and then] blend [them together as] a *Qetoret* [incense] compound, the work of a master perfumer, well-blended, free of all impurity, and holy. Pulverize a small portion of [the *Qetoret* daily] and place it [on the Golden Altar] before the [Ark of] Testimony in the Communion Tent where I commune with you. It shall have the highest degree of holiness for you [*Kodesh Kadashim*]. With regard to the *Qetoret* you are to make, do not duplicate its formula for your personal use. It must remain set aside for Yahweh. If a person makes it to enjoy its fragrance, he shall be cut off [spiritually] from his people (Exodus 30:34-38).

The Jewish Encyclopedia describes incense as "an aromatic substance which exhales perfume during combustion; the odor of spices and gums burned as an act of worship."

Incense was burnt ceremonially on an altar before the mercy seat in the Tabernacle. This particular formula for Holy Incense was made only for the worship of the Lord and required certain rituals in preparation.

According to the Temple Institute, "The method, or recipe, for preparing the special incense offering from was a closely-guarded secret, passed down from generation to generation within the ranks of one particular family known as Avtinas.

In addition to the identity of the spices and the exact amounts and manner in which they are prepared, the clan protected another important secret of their trade: The identity of an herb known in Hebrew as *ma'aleh ashan*, literally "that which causes smoke to rise." This herb has a quality which enabled the smoke from the incense to rise up to heaven in a straight column." It was forbidden to make Holy Incense just for pleasure of the senses.

Yahweh gave strict instructions how it was to be used in Exodus 30:1, 6-9:

> "And thou shalt make an altar to burn in-
> cense upon:....And thou shalt put it before the

vail that is by the ark of the testimony, before
the mercy seat that is over the testimony, where
I will meet with thee. And Aaron shall burn
thereon sweet incense every morning: when he
dresseth the lamps, he shall burn incense upon
it. And when Aaron lighteth the lamps at even,
he shall burn incense upon it, a perpetual incense before the LORD throughout your generations. Ye shall offer no strange incense
thereon, nor burnt sacrifice, nor meat offering;
neither shall ye pour drink offering thereon."

In Exodus 30:34-38, Yahweh provided a recipe from
which the incense was to be prepared:

"And the LORD said unto Moses, Take
unto thee sweet spices, stacte, and onycha, and
galbanum; these sweet spices with pure frankincense: of each shall there be a like weight: And
thou shalt make it a perfume, a confection after
the art of the apothecary, tempered together,
pure and holy: And thou shalt beat some of it
very small, and put of it before the testimony in
the tabernacle of the congregation, where I will
meet with thee: it shall be unto you most holy.
And as for the perfume which thou shalt make,
ye shall not make to yourselves according to the
composition thereof: it shall be unto thee holy

for the LORD. Whosoever shall make like unto that, to smell thereto, shall even be cut off from his people."

In this passage of Scripture, we find specific instructions on what ingredients are to be used in preparing the Holy Incense, how it is to be compounded, and are warned against using it improperly or treating it common. It should be simple in fact, to duplicate. But in reality, it isn't. After careful study of the names of each substance, the actual knowledge of what these ingredients are has been lost. Many different opinions, often contradictory ones have been set forth as to the identity of the ingredients in the Holy Incense. We will take a closer look and examine each one carefully.

According to the Torah, the *Qetoret* (Holy Incense) contained equal proportions of *Nataph*-Balsam/Stacte, *Shechelet*-Onycha, *Chelbenah*-Galbanum and *Levonah Zakah*-pure Frankincense.

While the Torah only mentions four main spices in the Holy Incense, it is recorded in the Sages of another seven, making a total of eleven spices according to the Oral Tradition. Rabbi Aryeh Kaplan gives a detailed explanation of how the extra seven are alluded to in the "terse language of the written Torah:"

"Since the Torah does not designate what they are, it seems obvious that the first mention of the word "spices" (after "take for yourself") would denote two different spices, since the minimum number that the plural form "*samim*" can be is two.

Then we have the balsam, onycha and galbanum, bringing us to a total of five. The Torah then mentions *samim* again to tell us that in addition to these five there were another additional five. This doubles the amount, making a total of ten. If the second *samim* only denoted two, the Torah would have said, "Take for yourself spices - balsam, onycha..."

Since the Torah divides them, it means that they were not the same. Therefore, the first time the word *samim* is mentioned denotes two spices; the second time it denotes five. Therefore, from the two times that the word *samim* occurs, we learn that there were seven spices besides the four mentioned in the Torah, making a total of eleven (see Kaplan, *Torah Anthology*, Volume 9, pp. 311-312)."

The *Mishnah* tells us the *Qetoret* was made up of eleven spices: "There were seventy measures each of balsam, onycha, galbanum, and frankincense. There were sixteen measures each of myrrh, cassia, spikenard, and saffron. There were twelve measures of costus, three measures of aromatic bark, and nine measures of cinnamon." In addition, other spices used to prepare the *Qetoret* included: nine *kabin* (quart) of Karshina lye which was used to rub the onycha with to make it more pleasant and three *se'in* and three *kabin* (quart) of Cyprus wine to soak the onycha in to make it more pungent. There was a fourth of a *kab* (cup) of Sodom salt, and a small quantity of smoke-producing herb. Jordan Amber, foam from the Jordan River was used to prevent the incense from sticking to the mortar and pestle. Rabbi Nathan of Babylon added, "If one omitted from or added to the original eleven spices, he was liable the death penalty."

The Torah does include very explicit instructions in the manner in which the *Qetoret* (Holy Incense) is used; in fact, if misused the punishment is *Karet*, or spiritual excision.

Because of its extremely exalted status, the Holy Incense was extra-carefully guarded and protected against misuse. The same is true of our prayer time, and manner in which we speak to the Heavenly Father.

The Holy Incense was considered *Kodesh*, meaning Holy in the Hebrew - to be set aside and kept separate. It then had the power to sanctify and elevate everything around it.

David likened his prayer to incense,

"Let my prayer be set forth before thee as incense; and the lifting up of my hands as the evening sacrifice." (Psalm 141:2).

The incense was considered holy because it represented the prayers of the saints and is a sweet aroma to Yahweh as described in Revelation 5:8:

> "And when he had taken the book, the four beasts and four and twenty elders fell down before the Lamb, having every one of them harps, and golden vials full of odours (incense), which are the prayers of saints."

Now, through prayer, the Bride of Christ has access to the throne room of Elohim through Yeshua, our High Priest:

> "Let us therefore come boldly unto the throne of grace, that we may obtain mercy, and find grace to help in time of need" (Hebrews 4:16).

Just as the Levite priesthood in ancient Israel was given a recipe in which to compound their Holy Incense, now believers as a "kingdom of priests" have been provided with a formula for prayer of four equal parts. They should be pure and come from a heart that longs to please God and follow His commands. Often our prayers are a sacrifice, especially when we fully submit to His will, and not our own.

Our high priest, Yeshua, gave us the model of prayer in Matthew 6:9-15:

> "After this manner therefore pray ye: Our Father which art in heaven, Hallowed be thy name. Thy kingdom come. Thy will be done in earth, as it is in heaven. Give us this day our daily bread. And forgive us our debts, as we forgive our debtors. And lead us not into temptation, but deliver us from evil: For thine is the kingdom, and the power, and the glory, for ever. Amen.

This example provides a structure for prayer covering those things that are important and pleasing to Yahweh. The Aaronic Blessing is another model for prayer. In it, it tells how to pray, not only what to pray.

And with this formula, our prayer should not be a mantra to be vainly repeated as many do (Matthew 6:7), but an outline of subjects to be considered (weighed and measured), expounded and discussed in person with our Heavenly Father in whom we have access.

The Sages tell us making the Holy Incense revolves around the ideas of retrieving, refining, extracting, and elevating the sparks of holiness and goodness, in ourselves and in the creation at large, from the unrefined state in which we originally received them.

The ingredients of the Holy Incense are the makeup of a well-balanced relationship with Yahweh through our prayer time.

We will now break down these four basic ingredients: *Tzori*-Balsam or Stacte, *Tziporen*-Onycha, *Chelbenah*-Galbanum, and *Levonah Zakah*-pure Frankincense and explore what should be included when we enter into the presence of our Heavenly Father.

Stacte

As the first ingredient of the Holy Incense, נָטָף *Na-taph* in Hebrew means "drop," corresponding to "drops of water" (Job 36:27). The English translations use Stacte, from the Greek word meaning "an oozing substance," referring to various viscous liquids including myrrh and labdanum (Rose of Sharon). Rabbi Gamaliel described it as "the sap that drips from the tapping of the wood of the *Ketaf* tree (Kerithot 6a). Rashi clarified, "*Nataph* is the same as *Tzree* (Balm), and since it is only drips (and is not drawn out), the drips from the *Ketaf* tree are called *Nataph* (drips). Interestingly, in the book of Jeremiah where *Tzree* is mentioned (Jeremiah 8:22, 46:11, 51:8), it was in concurrence with the root word *Refah*, meaning to heal. In other places in the Torah, *Tzree* (balm) is mentioned with spices that were carried by Ishmaelite traders in Genesis 37:25, and then in Genesis 43:11 as a gift from Jacob in the land of Canaan presented to Joseph, as the Prince of Egypt.

Gil Marks reported in his research concerning the *Qetoret* that, "some ancient sources indicate that *Nataph* and *Tzree* are not synonymous. Balm that exudes spontaneously (*Nataph*) was considered of the highest quality, as opposed to that produced through manmade incisions (*Tzree*); the latter acceptable for commercial purposes, while *Nataph* was specified in the *Qetoret*."

Some commentators claim Stacte to be the same as Myrrh, and there is sufficient evidence that the Greek *Stactae* was a form of myrrh. The Septuagint's mistake in translation could have been because both *Nataph* and *Stactae* mean "to drip" while myrrh was translated as מר, *Mor*, in the same chapter earlier in reference to the anointing oil. Almost all other commentators agree that the oozing matter comes from the balsam tree or one of the many types of storax trees– the sap being called "balm" in English.

Thousand years ago, in an oasis on the western shore of the Dead Sea numerous rare and special balsam trees sprouted from the terraces and hills of Engedi. The balsam oil from Engedi and Jericho was considered by the Greeks and Romans to be the finest in the world for its fragrance and as a medicinal salve. In fact, the city's name, Jericho, derived from the root *Rayach* (fragrance), alluded to the ancient presence of balsam trees in the area.

As a close relative to myrrh, author Gil Marks writes, "Varieties of balsam grew wild throughout much of the land surrounding the Red Sea. The one that produces the superior resin is *Commiphora opobalsamum*, a 10- to 12-foot high tree with a deep brown bark and small trifoliate leaves. During the heat and humidity of the summer, the aromatic resin spontaneously oozes out in drops from cracks in the lower section of the trunk, a process fostered with manmade incisions. The whitish balm gradually turns gray and solid. The still fluid sap may be added to oil, which absorbs the intoxicating fragrance. Solidified balm may be pulverized and added to oil or mixed with other resins. Balm, although very expensive, constituted a significant component of life in ancient Israel."

According to legend, balsam was originally brought to Israel from Arabia by the Queen of Sheba among her gifts to King Solomon. However, balm was already a prominent export from Canaan at the time of the Patriarchs in Genesis 37:25.

In 1996, the "Biblical Archaeology Review" reported that during the excavation of the ancient city of Gilead, they unearthed the remains of a building used for the manufacture of balsam essential oil. This oil known as the "Balm of Gilead" is noted in Jeremiah 8:22:

"Is there no balm in Gilead? Is there no physician there? Why then is there no healing for the wound of my people?"

This balm of Gilead was known for its miraculous healing of wounds. The production of this healing balm was so well guarded that archeologists found this inscription on the mosaic floor of an ancient ruin:

"Whoever reveals the secret of the village to the gentiles, the one whose eyes roam over the entire earth and sees what is concealed will uproot this person and his seed from the sun."

Just as the Stacte or storax gum exuded from the Balsam tree into liquid droplets and harden into 'tears,' those tears represent the tears shed in prayer, an example set by Yeshua himself, recorded in Hebrews 5:7:

"Who in the days of his flesh, when he had offered up prayers and supplications with strong crying and tears unto him that was able to save him from death, and was heard in that he feared."

Do we pray with Stacte? Do we shed unfeigned tears as we cry out to Yahweh for help? Do we shed tears of true repentance? What about the tears when we weep and mourn for what is happening around us in this world today as we pray for Yahweh's Kingdom to come, "Blessed are they that mourn: for they shall be comforted" (Matthew 5:4).

Onycha

Mystery and debate surrounds what is known as Onycha. Some believe it to be of plant origin, while others believe it to be from the finger-like operculum, or the closing flap of certain snails. Rashi, a great Jewish scholar, believed Onycha to be a kind of root that grew from the ground. Some suggest it is extracted from a Styrax benzoin, a type of resin used in the Tabernacle for incense in ancient biblical times. The Encyclopedia of Bible Plants (F Nigel Hepper 1992) agrees that onycha is more likely to be a plant resin. Rabbi Gamaliel (whom the Apostle Paul studied under) believed it to be part of the plant species and said, "The balm of Onycha required for the incense exudes from the balsam trees." The Jewish Talmud, whose Hebrew is of a later date than the scriptures, refers to the substance as *tsiporen*, which means fingernail and seems to be related to *sh'chalim*, meaning cress, a type of plant.

The Hebrew word for Onycha is שְׁחֵלֶת *Shecheleth* and refers to a resin with a nail-like shine, claw or hoof. For this reason, others believe it is an aromatic from the operculum of a shell fish, i.e., the claw or nail of the strombus or wing-shell, a univalve common in the Red Sea (the same mussel from which the blue dye for the Tzitzits (fringes) was obtained). The Greek word from the Septuagint 'onyx' also adds confusion. Onyx is an agate with a fingernail like opacity that has for some reason been associated with a claw shaped shellfish.

Onycha, as a plant derivative is highly aromatic and is credited as having great medicinal properties which seems to be the most likely ingredient for the sacred incense when considering the healing effect prayer has.

Tzori alludes to the Torah which is a balm that brings healing to the entire body. Onycha was valued anciently for its ability to speed healing of wounds and to help prevent infection.

Do we include onycha in our prayer by praying for those in need of healing? The Messiah had great compassion for the sick,

> "And Yeshua went forth, and saw a great multitude, and was moved with compassion toward them, and he healed their sick" (Matthew 14:14).

Yeshua also had compassion on those who needed spiritual healing,

"But when he saw the multitudes, he was moved with compassion on them, because they fainted, and were scattered abroad, as sheep having no shepherd" (Matthew 9:36).

Author of Apocryphal writings, Sirach compared Onycha and other sweet spices to the unfathomable wisdom of *Adonai* (Lord). It is important to pray for Israel's return to bring about that spiritual healing. As priests, we have been given the means by which to bring this healing about. Revelation 22:2 says, "the leaves of the trees were for the healing of the nations."

The Hebrew root for this spice comes from the root word *Shachal* meaning "to roar" or "a lion." Our Messiah and Savior, Yeshua has been given all authority in heaven and earth as the Lion of the Tribe of Judah (Matthew 28:18; Revelation 5:5). The fragrance of Onycha in the compound of the Holy Incense when offered on the altar serves as a reminder that Satan is a defeated foe. And, as disciples of Yeshua, we share in his power and authority "to tread upon serpents and scorpions, and over all the power of the enemy" in His name (Luke 10:19).

Galbanum

Resembling a giant fennel plant, Galbanum (Ferula galbaniflua, member of the carrot family) was used in the ancient world as incense. Native to the Middle East and grown in the Mesopotamian area and West Asia, Galbanum had to be imported in biblical times. Today it is cultivated in Iran, Turkey, Lebanon and Afghanistan.

Galbanum, also called "Mother resin," is discharged from the roots and lower trunk of this small wild plant. It is harvested by slitting its stem a few inches above the ground, allowing the milky substance to flow out and harden. Its balsamic tears are round, yellow to brownish-yellow, translucent, and not larger than a pea. It has been valued for its complex green, woody, balsam-like fragrance. At one time it was used in pharmaceuticals, but now it is mostly used as a food flavoring and as a perfume fixative. The Egyptians imported Galbanum resin in vast amounts, as it was a most treasured incense ingredient. In addition, Egypt used it for embalming and cosmetics.

The Jewish Talmud suggests that Galbanum, a bitter, earthy gum resin from an Asiatic plant was included in the Holy Incense because "Every communal fast that does not include the sinners of Israel is not a fast." This was because the Temple incense included spices with beautiful fragrances, but was considered incomplete without a less-than-fragrant aromatic such as Galbanum. Described by some modern Bible commentators as having a pleasant smell, Philo praises Galbanum, comparing it to air and calling it sweet smelling and says its smoke drives away serpents.

This sharp, biting pungent resin could be equated with some of the unpleasant things we need to pray about. We are required to examine ourselves carefully as we meditate on the Holy Scriptures,

> "Examine yourselves, whether ye be in the faith; prove your own selves. Know ye not your own selves, how that Yeshua Ha Mashiach is in you, except ye be reprobates?" (II Corinthians 13:5)

A genuine self-examination can be a very unpleasant experience. The Jewish Talmud say, *Chelbenah* alludes to complete sinners. Like a *Tziporen*-fingernail, they are smooth and unblemished on the inside, and only darkened on the outside.

In Hebrew, Galbanum is חֶלְבְּנָה *Chelbenah*. The Hebraic root is *Cheleb*, which means "the fat or the richest part" and *Chalab*, which means "milk." Of the animal sacrifices in Scripture, the fat was reserved for God and burned as a soothing aroma to Him (Genesis 4:4, Leviticus 3:14-16).

In the Greek, Galbanum is simply a borrowing of the Hebrew word, so there is no chance of error in translation from Hebrew to Greek. It is mentioned in the Egyptian papyri and only once in the Old Testament as an ingredient of the sacred incense and once in the Apocrypha (Sirach 24:15).

The fat was considered Yahweh's portion and was not for human consumption. Spiritually, fat is symbolic of praise and thanksgiving, followed by the confession of sins (Genesis 4:4, Leviticus 3:14-16). Psalm 50:23 says,

> "Whoso offereth praise glorifieth me: and to him that ordereth *his* conversation *aright* will I shew the salvation of God."

What joy it brings Yahweh when we come before Him with praise and thanksgiving and confess our sins and realize we are like filthy rags, unworthy and undeserving. Yahweh considers this His "*Cheleb.*" Hebrews 13:15 tells us,

"By him therefore let us offer the sacrifice
of praise to God continually, that is, the fruit of
our lips giving thanks to his name."

Geneva Bible notes explains, "Now that the physical
sacrifices are taken away, he teaches us that the true sacrifice
of confession remain, which consist partly in giving thanks,
and partly in liberality with which sacrifices indeed God is
now delighted."

Frankincense

Along the southern tip of the Arabian Peninsula comes the most prized Frankincense in the entire world. Grown high up on the grid plateaus, frankincense comes from a very low twisted bush-like tree that lacks a central trunk with it many prickly branches and pinnate leaves that extend every which way. Its sacred gum is obtained by slashing the roots and branches, making a deep incision then peeling back a narrow strip of its silvery bark, allowing the milky-white substance to ooze out. Once the air hits this substance, the sticky gum hardens into lumps. These lumps are either left on the tree for two weeks to dry or gathered and stored in mountain caves to dry for several months. Sap from the Frankincense is gathered until the middle of September, when rain showers ends the harvest season.

Caravans of camels carried this precious and rare spice packed in sheep and goat skins in quantities of 20 to 40 pounds through the bleak Arabian Desert, west along the Red Sea coast—a trip that takes months as described in Isaiah 60:6 and Jeremiah 6:20. In the Red Sea regions, Frankincense is not only valued for its sweet odor when burnt, but as a masticatory as blazing lumps of it are frequently used for illumination instead of oil lamps. Its fumes also serve as an excellent insecticide with its powerful bouquet, giving off no known toxicity.

Frankincense resins continue to be used for religious rites, medicines and perfumes. When combined together with other spices such as cinnamon or cassia, they create a myriad of scents. Its fragrant smoke that burned in censors was offered to guests to make clothes, hair or beards smell pleasant. The sweet vapor dispelled the unwanted scents of unwashed bodies, as well as refuse in the streets. It also served as an insect repellent, warding off infestation from the many sacrifices and offerings. Today, Frankincense is collected for use in the home as incense, cosmetics and perfumes, refinishing varnish, and chewing gum.

In biblical times, Frankincense was used for religious ceremonies. It was believed the prayers of the Cohanim (priests) on behalf of the people would ascend to heaven amidst the gentle wafts of incense. The Cohanim at the Temple in Jerusalem burnt a kilogram of incense each day with their prayers. The Scriptures record that Frankincense was burnt with other substances during the meat and flour offering (Lev. 6:15). In Leviticus 24:7 we read of how Frankincense was placed in purified form on the showbread in the tabernacle. Unlike the other ingredients of the Holy Incense, frankincense was also used in other parts of the Temple. It was specifically forbidden to add Frankincense to a sin offering, or to an offering to identify adultery, perhaps indicating its holy nature. The giving of this incense to Yeshua at his birth has been interpreted as symbolizing his priestly office (Exodus 30:34; Lev. 2:1,15-16; Matt.2:11). Historical documents reveal that the Queen of Sheba offered this prized aromatic gum to King Solomon. During Roman times, the Frankincense globules were worth there weight in gold.

This fourth and final ingredient, frankincense – in Hebrew is לְבוֹנָה *Lebownah* or לְבֹנָה *Lebonah* which means 'white light or pure,' indicating the color of the substance or the white smoke that it produces.

Lebonah Zakah alludes to Yahweh's love for His people through which He *me'laven*-whitens and bleaches our sins. We pray for our thoughts and deeds to be pure before Yahweh.

> "Draw nigh to Yah, and he will draw nigh to you. Cleanse your hands, ye sinners; and purify your hearts, ye double minded." (James 4:8)

How?

> "Casting down imaginations, and every high thing that exalteth itself against the knowledge of Elohim, and bringing into captivity every

thought to the obedience of Messiah;" (II Co-
rinthians 10:5).

Yeshua's priestly bride is anointed with the Holy
Spirit by our High Priest Yeshua, and should emanate this
from her wedding garments as well. Revelation 1:6 says:

> "And hath made us kings and priests unto
> God and his Father; to him [be] glory and do-
> minion for ever and ever. Amen."

Just as the Levites ministered to the Lord by burning
incense before the ark in the Holy of Holies, as it tells us in
Exodus 30:8, "And when Aaron lighteth the lamps at even,
he shall burn incense upon it, a perpetual incense before the
LORD throughout your generations," we too, must pray
without ceasing.

This white pillar of smoke that ascended, reaching
toward Heaven represented the prayers of the saints rising
before His throne. The book of Revelation 5:8 says:

> "And when he had taken the book, the four
> beasts and four [and] twenty elders fell down
> before the Lamb, having every one of them
> harps, and golden vials full of odors, which are
> the prayers of saints."

A portion of this prescribed incense was not burned but simply placed before the ark in the Holy of Holies. God said that this is "where I will meet with thee: it shall unto you most holy" (the holiest). Leviticus 24:7 says,

"And thou shalt put pure frankincense upon [each] row, that it may be on the bread for a memorial, [even] an offering made by fire unto the LORD."

Pure frankincense was placed on the loaves of bread (representing Yeshua) to symbolize the purity and fragrance of Christ, the true bread of God. We are reminded of Yeshua's words in John 6:32:

"Then Jesus said unto them, Verily, verily, I say unto you, Moses gave you not that bread from heaven; but my Father giveth you the true bread from heaven."

This portion represented the intercessory prayer made by Yeshua to the Father on our behalf and He continues to pray for you.

Chip Off The Ole Block

When all the ingredients of the Holy Incense are mixed together they produce something that is very precious, pleasing and holy to Yahweh.

The priests of ancient Israel gathered the ingredients, which were crushed to a powder, weighed out, mixed together and melted down into a large block which was more easily transported.

"And thou shall make it a perfume, a confection after the art of the apothecary, tempered together, pure and holy: And thou shalt beat some of it very small, and put of it before the testimony in the tabernacle of the congregation, where I will meet with thee: it shall be unto you most holy." (Exodus 30:36)

Each day the High Priest would chip off some of the solid block, crush it into fine powder and pour it over red hot coals to release the beautiful fragrant smoke.

Like that large block of incense, there is just so much to pray about that we cannot cover everything in one session.

In our own prayer time, all we can do is chip off a little each day and crush it to powder by getting down to the fine detail. By praying for specific events, individual people, their needs and well-being our prayers are refined, rather than praying in broad and meaningless statements. Seasoned with salt, our prayers are to be enduring, as a reminder of the perpetual covenant between God and Israel which He renews daily and confirms.

Should we see our lives on a "large" annual scale, or should we see them on a relatively "tiny" daily scale? The essence is to live each day to the fullest, paying attention to all the ingredients that go into making them up. This includes seeing the ingredients that don't smell so good as an important part of life.

And then, when we get to Rosh Hashanah or Yom Kippur, we can look back on a year full of full days. By Yom Kippur, our *Qetoret* (incense) will already have been ground and our prayer life is refined with knowing how to pray when we enter the throne room.

Holy Smoke

Just as the Holy Incense was to be burnt perpetually, we are to pray continually and be ready to pray at any time as needs arise,

> "Rejoicing in hope; patient in tribulation; continuing instant in prayer" (Romans 12:12).

Burning the resins on hot coals is reminiscent of the fiery trials we face from time to time. When the testing of our faith becomes difficult we immediately cry toward Heaven for help. And, like the heat of the coals that release the aroma of the incense instantly, our prayers in times of need are instantly released. This is when *Elohim* (God) turns a bitter experience into something sweet.

Teshuvah or true repentance is the ability to restructure a new life out of the raw ingredients we are given to work with and transform it into a sweet fragrance pleasing to Him.

And Yahweh is there, expecting our prayer and ready to "meet with thee" (Exodus 30: 6). When He hears our prayer, He responds. He gets great joy when we seek Him out in fervent pray,

> "Ointment and perfume (incense) rejoice the heart." (Proverbs 27:9)

The Torah states that this is the most powerful form of offering – because it has the power of life and death.

In the Midrash (Tanchuma, Tetzaveh 14), the letters of the word *Qetoret* can be read as an acronym: ק (Koof), ט (Tet), ר (Reysh) and a ת (Tav). This acrostic starts with the letter ק for קֹדֶשׁ *Qodesh*, which means holiness and the letter represents the back of the head or last. ט is for טָהֳרָה *Tohorah* which means purify and the letter ט means, to surround. ר is for רַחַם *Racham* which means Mercy and the letter ר means head or the highest. The final letter ת is for תִּקְוָה *Tikvah* which means hope and the letter ת means covenant, sign or cross. When you put it all together, it says:

> Koof (Behind/back of the Head - last)
> Tet (Surround)
> Resh (Head or the highest)
> Tav (Covenant, Sign, Cross)

He is the head of the body and it is his holiness that purifies us and surrounds us with His love. His mercy offers us hope and it is through His covenant on the cross that we can enter into His presence. Simply put, "Yahweh has got your back."

A Sweet Savor

Have you ever wondered why Yahweh did not want sweet fragrances or something more desirable in the Holy Incense? In Leviticus 2:11 it says,

> "You may not burn any leaven or honey as a fire-offering to Yahweh."

Leaven and honey both allude to pride. If honey is placed upon fire, it bubbles and rises more than any other liquid. Pride prevents one from recognizing one's faults and returning in true and sincere *Teshuvah* or repentance.

Our incense burnt on the altar with each of these prescribed ingredients in the Torah gives us the ability to be well-balanced in our relationship with Elohim.

By coming daily before His throne confessing our sins with sincere repentance that leads to the purification of thoughts and actions we can also pray effectively for the physical and spiritual well-being of others.

Our prayer will be answered:

"Confess your faults one to another,
and pray one for another, that ye may be healed.
The effectual fervent prayer of a righteous man
availeth much." (James 5:16).

In Hebrew, the word *Qetoret* describes something
that "rises up in circles, and whose aroma wafts and spreads"
(Keritot 6b). In Aramaic, the language of the Zohar, *Qetoret*
(similar to the Hebrew root *qesher*) means "connection,"
connection to the Divine. It has the power to elevate us and
bind us to our spiritual root (Zohar 3:11a).

And, isn't that what we all desire? When we come
before Yahweh to burn our incense in prayer daily, or in the
heat of fiery trial, we know that our prayers are heard by our
Father, and are considered precious and holy to Him.

The Importance Of Incense

The importance attributed to the offering of incense is apparent from the unique sanctity distinguishing the sacrifice. While it is the rightful privilege of the priesthood to offer it, II Chronicles 26:16 tells us how Uzziah the king was severely punished for audaciously taking upon himself this prerogative, suffering leprosy until his death.

The Torah itself denounces it as a sin deserving of death if anyone takes the *Qetoret* and uses it for common purposes, or even makes incense and duplicates it for purposes other than that prescribed by the law (Exodus 30:34-38).

The Old Testament records two tragic occurrences surrounding the *Qetoret*. In the first occurrence, Aaron's sons Nadab and Abihu, who were authorized Levites entitled to perform the service, perished when they profaned this most holy sacrifice by putting fire into their censers from another source (strange fire) instead of fire from the altar of burnt offering (Leviticus 10:1-2).

In the second occurrence, Korah and his company challenged Moses' and Aaron's authority in Numbers 16:6-7. Proving once and for all that his authority was God-ordained, Moses set up an ordeal involving, again, the *Qetoret*.

Moses told Korah in Numbers 16:6:

"the Lord will show who are His and who is
Holy; and will cause him to come near unto
him: even him whom he hath chosen will he
cause to come near unto him"

At the insistence of Korah, Moses instructed him
and his 250 men to come tomorrow with their fire pans and
place fire from the altar on them and offer the Holy Incense
before Yahweh. Korah refused to realize that the man
whom God had chosen had already been set-apart for this
purpose. This time the Sons of Levi had gone too far!

The next morning, Korah stood at the entrance of
the Communion Tent with his men, each one with an
incense pan in hand ready to offer the *Qetoret*. In an in-
stance, God's glory appeared and fire descended from
heaven. The earth opened up and swallowed them up and all
that pertained to them. The fire that descended from heaven
consumed the 250 men as well who had offered the *Qetoret*
(Numbers 16:18-34).

Unlike, many world religions with multiple gods and
temple priests, Moses warned those with the privilege of
serving Elohim must respect God's anointed *Cohen Gadol*
(High Priest). This appointment was made by God alone.

Interestingly, immediately after the matter of Korah, the congregation began to complain bitterly accusing Moses of killing God's people (Numbers 17:6).

Again, God's glory appeared in a cloud and spoke to Moses, warning that He would now destroy the people with a plague. Moses and Aaron fell on their faces, pleading for mercy. Then, Moses told Aaron in Numbers 16:46:

> "Take a censer, and put fire therein from off the altar, and put on incense, and go quickly unto the congregation, and make an atonement for them: for there is wrath gone out from the Lord: the plague is begun."

Aaron did as Moses commanded him and made an atonement for the people and stood between the dead and the living; and the plague was stayed. The incense that had brought death upon those who had misused it, now renewed life and saved the people from impending death and judgment.

> "And Aaron took as Moses commanded, and ran into the midst of the congregation; and behold, the plague was begun among the people: and he put on incense; and made an atonement for the people. And he stood between the dead and the living: and the plague was stayed. Now they that dies in the

plague were fourteen thousand and seven hun-
dred, beside them that died about the matter of
Korah. (Numbers 16:47-49).

For there is only one who is worthy of being our
Heavenly *Cohen Gadol* that has been set apart for this task,
namely Yeshua Ha Mashiach. Hebrews 5: 1 – 8 says,

> "For every high priest taken from
> among men is ordained for men in things per-
> taining to God, that he may offer both gifts and
> sacrifices for sins: Who can have compassion
> on the ignorant, and on them that are out of the
> way; for that he himself also is compassed with
> infirmity. And by reason hereof he ought, as for
> the people, so also for himself, to offer for sins.
> And no man taketh this honour unto himself,
> but he that is called of God, as was Aaron. So
> also Christ glorified not himself to be made an
> high priest; but he that said unto him, Thou art
> my Son, to day have I begotten thee. As he
> saith also in another place, Thou art a priest for
> ever after the order of Melchisedec."

During Yeshua's visitation here on earth, he offered up prayers and supplications with strong crying and tears to the Father on our behalf and continues to do so in Heaven as our High Priest. The book of Hebrews reminds believers that while he was in the flesh, he learned obedience by the things which he suffered and in doing so, he became perfect (fully mature) as the author of our salvation unto all them that obey him.

As a kingdom of Priests, our prayers should conform to the pattern set in God's Holy Word when we approach our Heavenly Father in Yeshua's name. Our prayers are hindered if we are not in fellowship with Yahweh or have sin in our daily walk.

Do you harbor unforgiveness toward a brother or sister in Christ? Are your prayers selfish, unclean or unrighteous? These things are considered "strange fire" to the Lord.

Incense In New Testament Times

After examining the Scriptures regarding the use of incense during Old Testament times, a new covenant believer may wonder if the *Qetoret* should be used today or if it was used in New Testament times. The answer is yes.

In the opening pages of the Gospel St. Matthew, the writer addresses the Messianic Jews living in Antioch, with the visit of the Magi (Wise Men from the Far East) who offered gifts of incense and gold to the young child. In Matthew 2:11 it says,

> "And when they were come into the house, they saw the young child with Mary his mother, and fell down, and worshipped him: and when they had opened their treasures, they presented unto him gifts: gold, frankincense, and myrrh."

The three gifts symbolized him as King, High Priest, and Suffering Servant. Gold, which is befitting for a king, Frankincense which is befitting for a High Priest / God (as an act of worship), and Myrrh which is befitting a suffering servant (as a resin commonly used for preparing bodies for burial), foreshadowing the suffering and bitterness of Christ's crucifixion.

These Oriental Scientists who studied Daniel's prophecies and the constellations understood that the promised Messiah was to be God in the flesh and bowed down to worship him with these significant gifts, just as the Holy One of Israel was to be worshipped with incense.

In Luke's letter to Theophilus we learn of a certain priest, Zacharias, of the course Abia. Lots cast had bestowed the great honor upon him of burning incense in the Temple of the Lord during the "hour of incense" (a common reference to the hour of prayer). While he was performing his priestly duties, an angel of the Lord appeared to him, standing at the right side of the altar of incense (Luke 1:5-25). This special messenger sent by God was Gabriel with the important news of the birth of John (forerunner to Christ) who would turn many hearts back to God, preparing the way for the Messiah.

The book of Acts also offers insight into the disciples continuing in the tradition of attending Temple at specific times when the incense was offered. In Acts 3:1, Peter and John heal a lame man at the Temple while on they way up to the hour of prayer/incense at the ninth hour (3pm). From the Old Testament scriptures such as Psalm 55:17 and Daniel 6:10, we know specific prayer times were observed while incense was being presented in the Temple. They are:

The First Hour (6am)

The Third Hour (9am)
The Sixth Hour (12 noon)
The Ninth Hour (3pm)

While some may criticize the regimen the First Century Apostles practiced, we are reminded in the book of Hebrews of the importance of the priesthood. Yeshua is now our High Priest, who sits at the right hand of the God the Father, and ministers in the true Tabernacle. Keep in mind that the Tabernacle Moses built was modeled after the one in Heaven (Hebrews 8:5). On earth, the Holy Incense was a continual reminder to God of the future restoration of all things in "thy kingdom come."

In order to take a glimpse into Heavenly worship, read Revelation 4:1 through 5:14. Here we see the twenty-four elders falling before the Throne of God in worship to the Lamb, each having a harp and golden bowls of incense, which are the prayers of the saints (Revelation 5:8). Again, we see incense mingled with prayers as a form of worship. In Revelation 8:3, we are told that an angel was given much incense and that the angel offered this incense with the prayers of all the saints upon the golden altar, which was before the throne. It says in Revelation 8:4,

"And the smoke of the incense which came with the prayers of the saints, ascended up before God out of the angel's hand."

Some may be ask, should the church be offering up prayers with incense as in the days of old or is it strictly forbidden without the proper Levitical priesthood or Temple in place? However, if angels in Heaven offer up the prayers of the saints with a golden censer of incense, should believers on earth model this or is it strictly symbolic? And, if our worship in the body of Messiah is to be a pattern after heavenly worship, should we as a kingdom of priests, be burning our incense before God? Careful consideration and prayer must be given to these questions.

Blessings Over The Fragrances

The majority of biblical scents used in the *Qetoret* were imported from countries such as Africa, Arabia and as far as China. Did God choose to use fragrances from foreign lands because he saw these spices as a prophetic foreshadow of how He would gather the nations unto Himself? In doing so, the herbs, resins and spices not having their origins in Israel speaks of God's intention to draw out of the nations those who would join Israel as a people that would bring a sweet savor of fragrant worship unto him? Selah.

As seen from Moses' blessing to the tribe of Levi in Deuteronomy 33:10-11, it is a premonition of wealth and success:

> "they shall put incense before thee; and whole burnt sacrifice upon thine altar. Bless, Lord, his substance, and accept the work of his hands…"

Each priest longed for the once in a lifetime opportunity to offer the *Qetoret* in the Temple, bringing great blessing upon his home and family.

Believers today can savor the sweetness of the Sabbath in keeping *Havdallah*, by passing spices as a reminder of the *Qetoret* for success in the coming week.

According to "The Complete Artscroll Siddur" every act and pleasure should be embarked upon with an awareness that it is God who is being served and it is He that meets our needs and desires.

Upon smelling the fragrances, recite this prayer:

Blessed are You, Hashem, our God, King of the Universe, Who creates species of fragrance.

Upon smelling fragrant shrubs and trees or their flowers:

Blessed are You, Hashem, our God, King of the universe, Who creates fragrant trees.

Upon smelling fragrant herbs, grasses or flowers:

Blessed are You, Hashem, our God, King of the universe, Who creates fragrant herbage.

Upon smelling fragrant edible fruit or nuts:

Blessed are You, Hashem, our God, King of the universe, Who places a good aroma into fruits.

As a remembrance of the *Qetoret*, the morning prayers mention the incense spices and how we are commanded to bring them before Yahweh:

It is You, HaShem, our God, before Whom our forefathers burned the Qetoret (incense-spices) in the time when the Holy Temple stood, as You commanded them through Moshe Your prophet, as is written in Your Torah.

The Avodah
(Adapted from the Rambam)

Rebecca At The Well Foundation

Rebecca at the Well Foundation is a non-profit Judeo-Christian organization devoted to inspiring believers to prepare for the return of the Messiah. By informing the "called out ones" the way to walk in the beauty of holiness, it motivates members of the body to be clothed with righteous acts and deeds as the Bride of Messiah.

In an effort to bridge the gap between Judaism and Christianity, Rebecca at The Well Foundation provides workshops and seminars about the Hebraic roots of our faith that binds us together as one. All believers can celebrate Yeshua's return as they learn how to make themselves ready as a pure and holy bride.

Rebecca Park Totilo, founder and president of the Rebecca at The Well Foundation, is currently touring the country, preparing the bride for her Heavenly Bridegroom. She is available to speak at conferences, seminars and retreats. Please contact her at (727) 688-2115 for more information, or if you would like to have her come and share with your group or congregation.

Visit our website at:
www.rebeccaatthewell.org or www.ratw.org

For e-mail correspondence:
becca@RebeccaAtTheWell.org

For snail mail correspondence:
Rebecca At The Well Foundation
PO Box 60044
St. Petersburg, FL 33784

Bibliography

Culi, Yaakov. Torah Anthology: Me'am Lo'ez. (Jerusalem, Israel: Maznaim Publishing Corp, 1979).

Kaplan, Aryeh. The Living Torah. (Jerusalem, Israel: Maznaim Publishing Corp, 1981).

Isaiah, Rabbi Abraham Ben and Sharfman, Rabbi Benjamin, Editors. The Pentateuch and Rashi's Commentary. (Brooklyn, New York: S. S. & R Publishing Company, 1950).

Neusner, Jacob. The Mishnah. (New Haven, Connecticut: Yale University Press, 1988).

Scherman, Rabbi Nosson. The Complete Artscroll Siddur. (Brooklyn, New York: Mesorah Publications, 1984).

Neusner, Jacob. Yoma, Trans.(Atlanta, Georgia: Scholars Press, 1994).

Brown, William. The Tabernacle: Its Priests and Its Services, Updated Edition. (Peabody, Massachusetts: Hendrickson Publishers, 1996).

Edersheim, Alfred. The Temple: Its Ministry and Services, Updated Edition. (Peabody, Massachusetts: Hendrickson Publishers, 1994).

Hutter, Terry Dr. Palynological Assessment of the Qumran Spices. (Jerusalem, Israel: Vendyl Jones' Report on the Excavations at Qumran, 1994).

Neusner, Jacob. The Midrash. (New York, New York: Jason Aronson Publishing, 1994).

Yohai, Shimon Bar. The Zohar. (New York, New York: Kabbalah Publishing, 2008).

Hepper, Nigel F. Encyclopedia of Bible Plants. (Downers Grove, Illinois: Inter-Varsity Press, 1992).

Walker, Winifred. All the Plants of the Bible. (New York, New York: Doubleday, 1979).

Becker, Udo. The Continuum Encyclopedia of Symbols. (New York, New York: Continuum International Publishing Group, 2000).

Strong, James, LL.D., S.T.D. The New Strong=s Exhaustive Concordance of the Bible. (Nashville, Tennessee: Thomas Nelson, 1990).

Wilkinson, Richard H. The Complete Temples of Ancient Egypt. (New York, New York: Thames & Hudson, 2000).

Encyclopedia Judaica. (New York, New York: Macmillan, 1971).

Cansdale, George. All the Animals of the Bible Lands. (Grand Rapids, Michigan: Zondervan, 1970).

Nielsen, Kjeld P. Incense in Ancient Israel. (Leiden: E. J. Brill, 1986).

Müller W.W. "Frankincense" in The Anchor Bible Dictionary (New York, New York: Doubleday, 1992).

Faulkner. The Ancient Egyptian Book of the Dead. (Austin, Texas: University of Texas Press, 1985)

Stern, David H. Complete Jewish Bible. (Clarksville, Maryland and Jerusalem, Israel: Jewish New Testament Publications, 1998).

The NIV/KJV Parallel Bible. (Grand Rapids, Michigan: The Zondervan Corporation, 1985).

Edidin, Ben M. Jewish Customs and Ceremonies. (New York, New York: Hebrew Publishing Company, 1941).

Spurgeon, Charles. Morning and Evening Devotional. (Rainbow Study Bible for Windows, Version 4.0B, 1996).

Matthew, Henry. Matthew Henry=s Commentary. (Rainbow Study Bible for Windows, Version 4.0B, 1996).

Earle, Ralph. Wesleyan Bible Commentary. (Kansas City: Beacon Hill Press), Luke, pp. 293-4.

Kolatch, Alfred J. The Jewish Book of Why. (Middle Village, New York: Jonathan David Publishers, Inc., 1981).

Internet Sources:

Morton, John. Burning Our Incense before God –
http://childrenofthepromises.org

Mienis, Henk K. Human uses of opercula –
http://manandmollusc.net/operculum_paul.html

The Hebrew Institute –
http://www.templeinstitute.org/incense.htm

JewishEncylopedia.com –
http://www.jewishencyclopedia.com/view.jsp?letter=I&arti
d=125

The Spiritual Significance of the Qetoret by Rabbi Avraham Sutton –
http://www.jewishencyclopedia.com/view.jsp?letter=I&artid=125

Spiritual Significance of the Incense –
http://www.jewishmag.com/11mag/mystic/mystic.htm

The Talmud –
http://www.jewishvirtuallibrary.org/jsource/Talmud/talmudtoc.html